TABOO

Tori Lynn

Book Cover by Earl Dixon - On Point Graphic Design

Editing by Faleasha Smith-Tate

Most of the Bible scriptures in this book have been quoted from the BibleHub.com website these are other versions that were used.

New Living Translation (NLT)

New International Version (NIV)

God's Word Translation (GWT)

The information inside is for entertainment purposes only. Content should not be used to replace any professional, medical, legal, or financial advice.

Published by
AuthorToriLynn.com &
LikeMinds

ACKNOWLEDGMENTS

To my Heavenly FATHER!!!! YEEEEESSSSSSSSS YOU ARE SO AWESOME!!! YOU continue to amaze me. I'm smiling and feel YOU smiling back even while I type. Thank you!!!!

A special THANK YOU to all who were part of the Survey, poll, opinions and stories. Your openness and honesty will dearly help someone else.

To my family, friends, social media family, thank you for your support.

To Aunt Sandra Steele who continues to encourage me. God gave the gift of exhortation and everyone around you knows it. I hope when I approach seventy, I have a body like yours and diva-tude. "Work it!" Love Tink.

Grandma, so many words have come back to me, in a nut shell, "Be a Freak!" I so wish you were here to Co-Author <u>TABOO</u> with me because I could use your wisdom.

To my mom, author, playwright, speaker, Jerri Lynn, you are the strongest woman I know. Thank you for the funny parts you allowed me to use. (You missed your calling as a comedian.)

To my brother/son Scottie, I'm so proud of the man you have become. You have beat the odds. Your time is coming sweetheart.

Last but not least, to my girls: The authors, actresses, singers, and entrepreneurs Erin Lynn and Ryan Lynn. The best compliment is being your mommy. The encouragement I get from you two, "You're the Best Mommy ever" and/or when you say that to your friends and "I wish your mommy was my mommy."   There were so many times I felt guilty because we moved to Atlanta and six months later we became homeless and ended up in a shelter, AGAIN. THROUGH ALL OF IT, you two kept your Faith in GOD & still adore your mommy. I love u.

TABLE OF CONTENTS

"...The World is taking half y'alls men!"

I had been waking up every morning at 5:52 a.m. thinking about sex. Not in a lustful way, but in the way of passion. So, I spoke to a few of my friends about it:

First I spoke with Lisa, ten year live-in relationship with boyfriend.

Me: "Hey Lisa, I think God wants me to write another book."

Lisa: "You better get started!"

Me: "But I think it's on sex. Why would HE have me write a book on sex when I'm Christian, single, and celibate?"

Lisa: "Because the world is taking half y'alls men!"

Then I spoke to my friend Dawn: "I believe God is having you to write this book. Because the Bible said that the older women are supposed to teach the younger women. My daughter Nicki, has been married for three years but doesn't really enjoy sex with her husband, but doesn't know what to say to make her feel comfortable because I'm her mother. Nicki admitted: "A couple of my friends and I have always been taught that sex is bad, how to be 'Good Girls,' and don't do it, but now that we're married, we really don't know what to do, or what we are or not supposed to do."

Jess, my bisexual buddy.

Me: "Jess, I think God wants to write a book about sex."

Jess: "Because half the Christians I know are hypocrites. They act like they don't have sexual feelings or sex is wrong."

I asked these people particularly because I didn't want the cliché.

ATTENTION: This book is an inspirational/self-help that has collections of surveys, polls, and stories from men and women from ages 38-68. I wanted more than my experiences, opinions, perspectives and suggestions in this book. Enjoy!!!

MARRIAGE QUOTES

"Marriage is not hard, it's just work."
-R. and D. Allen married over 45 years

"Marriage is not hard, it's like a heart; it **has to** beat. It cannot take a break or quit because it gets old or tired."
 —Fails Happily Married over 24 years

"The best part about being married is Companionship."
-Happily Married for 50 years, 3 grown sons

"Once our kids are grown and gone, we will still do the things we do now because we're best friends." L. and L. Allen married 18 years, parents of 6 grandparent 1½.

"My wife is my best friend. I can do a lot of stuff with my boys but I really have fun with my wife." Husband of 3

"I like it when my husband holds my hand when we hang out." Wife

 "We can improve our relationships with others by leaps and bounds if we become encouragers instead of critics." - Joyce Meyer

"If your husband wants you to come to bed in lipstick, put on the LOUDEST RED that you can find." Patricia Ashley

CHAPTER 1

IT'S ABOUT THAT SEXY!!!

Ok, let's start this off right here, EVERYONE HAS A SEXY!!!

When I asked around (men and women) what makes a person sexy? Unanimously, the answer was CONFIDENCE. Of course, there is the physical pulchritude, but CONFIDENCE was usually the first answer. Confidence is Sexy.

When a person leaves from their mirror in the morning, their mirror will show and tell them what everyone else will see. If you have a boogie hanging onto your mustache, or if your mirror shows you a panty print. So you should be confident in what your mirror show and tells you because others may lie but a mirror won't.

When a man walks into a room, you can tell where his confidence is. It's the way he holds his head and shoulders; same as a woman. If he or she walks with their head down, minimal eye contact, or slumped, that's where that person is located.

You can be sexy without being a slut or pervert. You can be sexy without setting off a spirit of lust. For example: a nice pair of jeans that can be fitting to show your shape but if it's giving camel toe, or looks as if they've been painted on or too tight you can send the wrong signal. Plus it can cause a yeast infection. Soon you will have an OOCHIE Coochie!!!

Husbands, pay attention, women go through a cycles, and one is called the Ovulation cycle. Studies show that during this time is when the husband finds his wife very sexy (Chapter 11 is on Ovulation). Now, there are women who have passed the fertile years but don't worry, men think it's sexy because it's a relief that they don't have to "pull-out," there is no "time of the month" that he can't get sex, no pregnancy scare, and they don't have to nor use condoms on his wife. That is sexy on its' own.

I understand, sometimes, when we are going through, or have gone through weight gain, depression, divorce, and/or loss we want to see if we still, "got it."

Ladies my current size is 211lbs. What I have found is men are attracted to sexy. Period. Now there are some that prefer a certain size, but they still like sexy. I prefer to date my African-American brothers, but I must admit, it's fun seeing other nationalities respond to me when I walk by. Men respond to sexy and confidence.

I asked a few guys about their preferences for weaves, lashes, relaxers, naturals, nails, and toes. Many preferred natural but appreciate the woman who keeps herself together.

What is your sexy???

If you don't know what your sexy is, what are you most complimented on? What's that "thing" that even when your spouse is upset, that "thing" is still sexy about you? I know that's not a term that some of you would use for yourself so think about something what you've heard people compliment you on: eyes, complexion, teeth, smile, boobs, hips, chest, waist, hair, thighs, mustache, legs, height, smile, lips, etc.....

What's your Handsome/Beautiful?

Not being conceited, it's just something I know I have, great eye lashes and eyebrows. According to my grandma, "You better know it first! Everybody can think it, everybody can see it but if you don't know it..." Every person should KNOW what their sexy is. Think about it, what's that "thing" that even when your spouse is upset with you, that "thing" is still sexy?

Wherever you may feel you lack confidence, what do you do to make-up for it? You accentuate your "thing." For instance, I know a guy who is short; but, he has beautiful full shaped and soft lips and he knew it. He was sexy because of his confidence.

If there is something you would like to see on your mate, you have to subtly and carefully bring it to their attention. Example: My friend and I were leaving a movie and

I complimented a guys' hair cut to my date as we passed him. I wasn't disrespectful with it, it was a simple complimented it. Now be careful not to exalt another man over your husband, not even a pastor.

Sometimes, there is a sexy "thing" that someone else may see in us that we either have never noticed, too shy or reserved to explore and it takes the right person to pull it out; if you're willing to play with the notion. One thing a guy did for me, without asking, was bought a dress for me to wear to an All Black Party.

Me personally, I thought the dress was a bit tight and short for my taste, and I told him. Now I could go for tight, or short, but tight and short! He said, "Just try it on. If you don't like it, then..." I knew and trusted that he would never put me in anything that would embarrass himself nor me. He wasn't into trashy, and I'm into sexy classy so I got dressed and came into the room where he was. He looked at me with the BIGGEST grin and said, "YOU LOOK BEAUTIFUL! YOU LOOK SEXY!" He was right. He, along with my mom, had been trying to get me to be a little sexier. I'm used to being a little more conservative, but this was fitting for a party I had that "Sexy Classy" thing going. Would I dress like that all the time, maybe not, but this time I did and I did it for him. At one point through the night he leaned to me and said, "I feel like I have the 'baddest girl in the game wearing my chain.'" I could tell he enjoyed the compliment of watching other men look at me.

(Wives, be careful with your hair. Do not go and do a BIG CHOP without notifying your husband first. It's not that you need permission, it's out of respect. Remember your body no longer belong to just you and out of respect you may want to at least run it by him.)

1 Corinthians 7:4 NIV – The wife does not have authority over her own body but yields it to her husband. I the same way, the husband does not have authority over his own body but yield it to his wife.

CHAPTER 2

WHO ARE YOU???

Do you know who you are? There was a time that a lady asked our class, I was probably in middle school or high school, "If you could describe the world, how would you describe would you describe it?" There were many different answers: One person said, "The people are mean," someone else said, "There are lots of flowers," someone else said, "Tired, everybody is tired," and so on. The reason for the question was because how you see the world is really a reflection of yourself.

Wow, that was so profound. I began to have fun with it and asked others. The best answer I had gotten was when I asked a man, "I see the world as one big ball of confusion." And to be honest, some people thought he was a little crazy or confusing man. I laughed at that for about two months.

My point for asking that is because, we have to know ourselves. How do you see yourself? And, how do others see you? Are you considered a negative person or a positive person? Are you known to be mean or fairly easy-going? Do people call you lazy or a go-getter?

Sometimes we just have to get real. If it walks like a duck, and quack like a duck, it's a duck. If you hear negative comments a lot like, "You are very nice person until you get angry." Or, "You go from 0 to 100 in seconds." Everyone is not picking on you. Especially if this behavior gets you into trouble. Get checked out. There's help for it.

There's something called mental health: Bipolar, Schizophrenia, Depression, Paranoia, sex addicts, alcoholic and etc. If you go into a relationship, you can go in telling your potential mate that there's a condition that you deal with and may require patience and prayer. I believe this is something that should be disclosed up front and allows the potential mate to see if this is something they can handle.

This may be something that can lift some of the divorce rate. Know who you are. Be fair. It's okay because no one is Jesus, and everybody has something they deal with.

Survey says...

What You Won't Do...

Women need <u>Affection</u> and <u>Communication</u>

Husbands, Talk! Send a morning text from work, compliments, get back in the car and hand her a flower you just bought while paying for gas, have "Just because I love you" flowers delivered, or you deliver, to her job, surprise with favorite snack, pay attention, even notice that her hair is parted differently. (If she doesn't like flowers, there are other great things you can surprise her with: favorite perfume, fruit basket, a picnic...

The examples represents communication and affection.

DO NOT get caught slipping by allowing another man to show **your wife** some type of affection.

Another Will Do!

Men need <u>Sex</u> and <u>Peace</u>

Wives, Don't Talk! Initiate sex, send a morning text, a surprise "quickie" visit (wink), the "Big Daddy" text, send sexy picture of lingerie (wink, be creative), initiate sex, be spontaneous, wink at him from across the room, try something new in the bedroom, keep lights on, get Lavender and Vanilla massage oil, feed him (wink), Initiate sex, cook for him, serve him, rub him, kiss him, shock him, don't talk, initiate sex...

The examples above represent Sex and Peace.

QandA

Me: "When your wife retired from the military, she gained a little weight, how did you feel about her weight gain and did she change (self-esteem) because of it?"

Mr. RL: "Well, her weight gain doesn't matter to me because she still look good. She still dresses nice. She hasn't really complained about her weight and she still looks good. When people compliment my wife it makes me feel good. I like to hear it."

Me: "Are you still turned on by her now just as you were before the weight gain."

Mr. RL: "Yeah, She's my wife; she's my best friend. She has my back. After 23 years we are still intimate a few times a week! All she has to do is pooch up."

-R.L. Husband of 23 years

CHAPTER 3

HOW THE SEXUAL ADDICTION STARTED

When I was three years old, I was molested by an older family member. When I was six, I was molested by a teen, who was around fifteen years old and worked for my mom and step dad's janitorial business. I was between nine and eleven, when I molested by a nephew of my mothers' male "friend," who was about ten years older than me. All these people, I KNEW, and was very comfortable with so at a very early age, I learned that boys liked for girls to put their penis in a girls' mouth. I didn't know why but they enjoyed it, it warranted strong reaction, and obviously felt good because each guy wanted the same thing.

The three-year-old molestation was the one that haunted me for years because of where it happened, a place that I visited very often because it was a family member. The other two males, 15 years old and 18 years old, don't remember much about them except I knew them personally. I never told my mom about the molestations. Maybe because of the attention I was given. Although my innocence was taken at such an early age, the act was quite fun, so I thought.

As young as I was I knew it wasn't something I was supposed to do, yet guys enjoyed it. I really don't know how I knew to keep it a secret, or if it was a secret. As I grew in years, kissing, licking, and touching on each other, as kids, was no big deal. "Playing House," "Playing mommy and daddy," "Doing it," etc. seemed to be the thing to do at sleepovers. Maybe that's why it didn't seem a bad thing, everybody was doing it. No one told me at an early age not to play those types of games or not to touch and feel on others nor let others touch and feel on me. All the while, it was going on.

Around middle school age, I remember my first boyfriend who I snuck in the house while my mom was gone. He and I were kissing and using our fingers and hands when suddenly I went down. Again, strong reaction. Come to think of it, that's how the other two situations happened with Jason and Rod. Maybe I wasn't molested after all since it was something I had initiated. No! I was only six and nine. They knew better. I was a kid, and they should have taken control and not allowed it nor allowed a kid access to it. Nevertheless, I was addicted to oral sex before the age of nine.

My family could not figure out my "bad girl" behavior. I never told my mom what had happen to me until I was sixteen.

PREVENTIVE MEASURES:

Take preventive measures immediately. Molestation, rape, sodomy, and incest has NO beginning and it has NO end date. It can happen to anyone, at any time, at any age, by anyone, and with anything. So, because I was molested at the tender age of three, I started teaching my daughters, while they were still in diapers, **"This is YOUR private, NOBODY PLAY! NO, NO."**

When they were old enough to talk, I often told them, **"This is YOUR PRIVATE and NOBODY TOUCH YOUR PRIVATE. YOU SAY NO, NO!**

Around 3 or 4 years old, I googled and showed them pictures of mouths with blisters. **"THIS IS WHAT HAPPENS IF SOMEONE TOUCHES YOUR PRIVATE AND MOUTH, IF YOU TOUCH SOMEONE ELSE'S PRIVATE AND MOUTH, OR YOU LET SOMEONE PUT THEIR MOUTH ON YOUR PRIVATE OR MOUTH. NO, NO!"**

Take preventive measures EARLY because if that (Generational curse) comes for your child, they may respond better than you because you prepared them.

PROTECT YOUR CHILD 1ST BY TEACHING THEM TO PROTECT THEMSELVES, SO THEY WILL KNOW WHAT TO SAY IF DANGER PRESENTS ITSELF. THEY WILL RESPOND BECAUSE THEY WERE TAUGHT.

Mark 9:42 NLT "But if you cause one of these little ones who trusts in me to fall into sin, it would be better for you to be thrown into the sea with a large millstone hung around your neck.

CHAPTER 4

RUG BURN

Erica's mother, Lisa, was a good person and provider. She loved all her children and accepted anyone into her home church. Chrystal's mom, Felicia, and step-dad Jeff, had been married six years and were very active and respected in the community. We all came from middle-to-upper class lifestyles, has had the best of everything, and took many vacations. Erica was crazy about her mom and would do anything for her. Chrystal tolerated her step-dad and had a lack of respect for her mom; and it was obvious.

They say, "Birds of a feather flock together." Well, Erica, who I had just been friends for less than six months, and Chrystal, who I had known for three years), had sexual addictions as well. We did a lot of things, and knew a lot about each other without judgement. One night we had been out partying and drinking with some of our other friends. Sure enough we were too drunk to drive home and ended up sleeping over at the party. The next morning, well afternoon, still hung over, we stopped and had breakfast. While sitting in the restaurant, we began to talk about our hilarious night. We laughed and joked but eventually it got serious, we all found that we had been molested. We took our food to-go because I saw that Erica was having a moment and I didn't want her to be embarrassed. Shoot, I didn't want to be embarrassed just in case I joined her with tears.

We stopped at the liquor store and picked up Sprites and gin. When we arrived at Chrystal's apartment complex she invited us in and wanted to continue our conversation. We were still pretty hungover but as we talked, we started drinking again while Erica smoked a joint. I don't remember how we began talking about being molested but here is a story, put with another's emotions. (Thank you ladies for allowing me to share.):

"When I was fifteen, at about 5 o'clock in the morning, I was asleep when I began dreaming: It was bright outside and I was lying down on concrete, when I felt something. I looked down and there were an army of fire ants crawling up my leg and into my nightgown. I suddenly **woke up** out of that dream and realized that it wasn't ants. It was my stepfathers' hand going up my leg raising my nightgown. Startled, he hurried and slid through the cracked door and out of my room. I couldn't go back to sleep because I was afraid he'd come back. My heart was pounding so hard that my nightgown vibrated.

That morning while mom drove me to school, I told her what happened:

Chrystal: "Mom, Jeff was in my room last night."

Mom: "Why? What was he doing?"

I told her what happened and her response was: "You said you were asleep?"

Chrystal: "Yes"

Mom: "So you are sure he was in there?"

Chrystal: "Yes."

Mom: "How do you know you weren't dreaming?"

Chrystal: "Because I woke up and saw him slide through the door."

Mom: "But it was dark in your room, right?"

Chrystal: "Yes."

Mom: "Did you say anything to him?"

Chrystal: "No, I was too scared."

Then my mom said those dreadful words: "Okay, I'll ask him about it when I get home."

I went through my day dreading the conversation to come, because I knew what his answer would be and she'd have to choose who to believe. If she chose to believe me, she may have to sacrifice being married, and possibly take further action; or, if she chose to believe him, he'd have a secret, he would've gotten away with his act, and would possibly do it again.

When mom picked me up from school our conversation continued.

Mom: "Chrystal, I had a talk with Jeff and he strongly denies being in your room last night."

Chrystal: (not shocked and looking down) "Mom, he was in my room, raising up my gown."

Mom: "And you said you didn't say anything?"

Chrystal: (Realizing that she didn't believe me; OR, she **didn't want to** believe me) "No."

Mom: "And the room was dark?"

Chrystal: "Yes."

Mom: "Are you sure you weren't dreaming. Because he says he was not in there."

Chrystal: (Beginning to second guess myself) "You know what mama, I may have been dreaming."

Mom: "You think so?"

Chrystal: "Yes."

Mom: "Okay, we won't talk about it anymore."

Erica added, "When I told my mom that my uncle raped me, he denied it and she asked me why would I accuse him of something so evil. Why the hell would I make something like that up? Yes he's a minister but I'm her daughter. She cares about what other people think more than she cares about me and calling him out! Hypocrites!"

I added, "Things I did for sex: I remember sneaking boys in the house, ditching my first period of school, forging my mother's signature for school so I could leave for sex, being dropped off at the movie theater, jumping in a waiting car with a boyfriend, tried a threesome, sex in the cars, and etc. There was no limit, I had to have it."

When it's "Swept Under The Rug"

Feelings and emotions expressed, "I learned that I could possibly be crazy, to second guess, and not to trust **myself**." "Sadly, when I learned about the Doubting Thomas, (John 20:24-27) I totally related to losing faith." "My value, my self-esteem, and my self-worth was stripped, and my feelings no longer mattered." "That God-given confidence of protection that a child has in a parent, had died." "I had been told not to talk about it anymore; so, I learned to "Suffer in Silence."

Some rug burns are medicated with drugs, sex, and alcohol.

CHAPTER 5

WHY DOESN'T MY WIFE WANT TO HAVE SEX ANYMORE?

One day the salon was slow so I went outside and sat in the car with my grandma, who refused to get out of the car because she was working on a crossword puzzle. So, I was following up on a Q and A that I had previously posted on Social Media. Of course, whenever you're posting about sex many will gladly chime in and give their advice and opinions.

At one point I received an inbox from Paul, "Tori, will you ask this question but please don't put my name on it. It's embarrassing but what can I do to get my wife to perform oral sex on me." So, I posted the question and there were the advice and comments coming.

Grandma looked over at me and asked, "Tori, what are you doing?"

I answered, "I have a discussion going and a guy asked how to get his wife to perform oral sex on him, and there are many comments on the post but there are people who have also inboxed their suggestions, and I'm posting those who want to stay anonymous."

She asked, "What's the question?"

While typing my question to the post, I answered her, "Well, there's a guy who wants to know what he can do to get his wife to perform oral sex on him. There are a lot of people responding with good tips."

Grandma questioned, "Has it always been that way or did she suddenly stop?"

I responded, "I don't know but reading between the lines it sounds like she stopped."

She stopped her crossword puzzle and retorted, "You can get all the advice on there but the real reason she stopped is because she doesn't like him anymore."

I looked at her and asked, "Wait, what? How do you know? Huh???"

She continued, "ToTo think about it, we (women) don't touch things that we don't like. Now, he needs to go back and find the WHY. There's something he's done, and now he needs to go back to when was the last time she performed on him. We don't just stop doing something that we know our husbands like. There's a WHY. He needs to find it and fix it."

CHAPTER 6

HEART to HEART

HER HEART

The quickest way for a wife to lose respect for her husband is if she doesn't feel that she's number one in his life, valued or secured in the relationship by him. Women grow up watching fairytales and other movies where there is a damsel in distress rescued by a prince or a Knight in shining armor: Cinderella was valued, rescued, and secured by a Prince, Jazmine was rescued by Aladdin and Fiona was even rescued by an Ogre, Shrek. The story in <u>Beauty and the Beast</u> when the Beast rescued Belle from the wolves. Although these were fictitious stories, as children we bought into the notion that there really is a "True Love's Kiss" that we'll be rescued, and we will live Happily Ever After.

Many men wonder why they are in the "friend zone." Can this be changed? YES!!! The reason we put men in the friend zone because an emotional need most women have to have is **Protection**. She has to know that she's safe when she's with you, even if it's the smallest thing, you will speak up for her.

Example: A gentlemen had taken me out to eat for my birthday. This guys' demeanor was docile and meek, which could be mistaken for weakness. He had taken me to one of my favorite seafood restaurants for my birthday and they didn't put enough sauce on the Salmon Yvette dish that I had ordered. Obviously he was paying attention to how I was trying to spread the sauce around and asked me was everything okay. I answered yes, but he could tell it wasn't. He asked for the waiter and said, "Tell him what you need." Then, I was able to get more sauce. The point for me making this example was this gentlemen paid attention to the smallest thing. Sauce??? I could have enjoyed the meal without extra sauce, but I like the feeling that I felt at that moment; this meek man spoke up for me. (Matthew 7:7 Ask, and it shall be given to you.)

Another thing this guy did that moved him from the "friend zone" was he didn't quit. He was a very patient gentlemen, and he pursued me; he would not quit until he got his trophy. I realized this man was not a quitter. It was SEXY.

We were together for a few years but it didn't last because I never got Daddy from him. He was and is a good man but I had young daughters who were fatherless and wanted or needed a daddy. He was a provider, he took great care of them and was in tuned to their needs as well but he just wasn't the, snuggle up on the side of daddy, "in-touch-with-his-feminine-side," walk in the door run and hug daddy. He told me that his dad was the same way. He really did not get a lot emotionally nor much interaction from his father. He was a great father, provider, and protector but just not Daddy.

There are many women who were, either raised by a dad or a father figure, and usually, that's her first taste of how a man is to treat a woman; many girls develop the Electra Complex. Nine times out of ten, she will later marry a man who is very similar to the male model she had growing up, good or bad. Also, how she saw how a man treated her mother, or how she allowed a man to treat her will also be normal. Those norms follow us. Mothers, remember that when you are choosing a mate, choose the mate for yourself that you would choose for your daughter because she's watching and this will be her norm and the model to mimic.

As I mentioned in **The Divorce**, towards the end of our marriage, I felt my ex-husband did not protect me from his family. Whatever we went through was not for his family to know and when he and I had our problems, he began to tell them and them our text fights. I had part in this too, his mom wanted me to confide into her versus my family because, "If you talk about your problems to your family, when you two make up, they will still be angry and nothing you could do will restore it." She was right except I confided, along with her son (who warned me to not talk to his gossiping mom), to her and the "tight" relationship between his mom and me changed for the worse after a while and there was nothing he could do to restore it when he came home.

In the downward spiral of our relationship, I continued to have sex with my husband I was physically there but not emotionally. One day while having sex he asked, "Who are you thinking about?" The two reasons I continued to have sex with him were: I like sex and I had an obligation as a wife. But he was right, I was having sex with my husband while thinking about a past relationship where I felt adored and valued.

SEX IS MENTAL for women. If we're tired, stressed, overwhelmed, overworked, devalued, feeling unappreciated, feeling like the "man of the house," or even feeling alone good luck with getting us to initiate sex, become aroused, or get wet. We love feeling like Cinderella; pursued, captured, and worth it. (Jacob worked 14 YEARS for Rachel. Gen 29:20)

My friend Raven, wanted more sex from her man. She voiced that to him countlessly. She went and got a toy, which was cute at first, then he began to resent it. Eventually, she stepped out. Finally, she left him for someone else.

GREAT QUOTES

"When we were younger, mama cheered us on for everything. What we men can't figure out is why you stopped!?" Bishop T.D. Jakes series titled, <u>Fight for the Family</u>. One of the BEST Sermons EVERRRRR!!!!!!!!!

"MEN NEED SEX and WOMEN NEED AFFECTION!" - Myles Monroe

A woman should always smell like a fragrant. If a man smells her neck, he should ALWAYS smell a fragrant, even if it's faded from earlier." - Fred Hammond

"Women marry men hoping they will change, Men marry women hoping they will not." Albert Einstein

HIS HEART

One thing we know about our heavenly, Father is that He is a jealous God. (Exodus 34:14, 20:3, 20:5, Deuteronomy 4:24, Joshua 24:19, you get the point.) He inhabits our praise. If we don't praise Him, the stones will cry out. (Luke 19:40) Hmm, sound familiar? Like Father, like son. Yes, men have it honest. So, when we validate or praise any man over our husbands, they get jealous and it began to be a slow eating cancer. Yes, men get into their feelings and sometimes seek validation elsewhere.

Obviously, Delilah showed resplendent respect for Samson. (Judges 16) He knew she was scheming, yet, the validation and admiration she gave kept drawing him back like a magnet. Hmm, sounds like how some affairs are born.

Men need to feel like men, respected as men and spoken to like men. Although a wife may feel she doesn't NEED her husband, she should never make him feel that way. He HAS to feel needed. Just because they're in male bodies doesn't mean they don't have feelings or should just "take it because he's a man." Some men have certain fears just as women do. Now I wouldn't recommend that he be a cry baby, or considered a "Mama's **Boy**, (most grown men don't want to be called **boy** anyway) but he should able to feel safe with his wife as Proverbs 31:11 NLT Her husband can trust her and she will greatly enrich his life.

I promised "To love, to honor, and to respect..." but I am guilty of something. I married a man who I expected to change once I married him, and when he didn't I lost respect for him.

Men need to feel appreciated; just like they were when they were younger. GOD has commanded that women submit to husbands. Now we have a new age of women, women movements, and "I am women hear me roar." But GOD told us to submit to our husbands. (Ephesians 5:22, 23) at the Eve was chosen to be the helpmeet, not the head of the man. He was the protector over earth and everything in it (Gen 2:15). This is why God commands us to submit. It was to have order, as a business do. When there is a business, usually there is one CEO. The success or failure of the business depends on the CEO. When there are decisions to be made, the FINAL decision is made by the head/CEO. As Adam and Eve, Adam was the one who was told BY GOD not to eat from the tree knowledge of good and evil (Genesis 2:17, 18), not Eve. And, Adam moved out of his Birthright by allowing Eve to take his place as the head and he submitted to her will, by eating the fruit that **he was told, by GOD,** not to; so when they sinned, God came for Adam.

This leads me back to submission, GOD had man to be the protector and CEO. This is why men become very aggravated when he is not respected as the head. Yet, when a man gives up his position, it is hard for the woman to submit to him, and usually when a man doesn't know who he is, where he should be, or not walking in his position, she loses respect for him.

When a man doesn't take responsibility, makes excuses, blames others, she loses respect for him. *Genesis 3:12* NIV *The man said, "The woman you put here with me--she gave me some fruit from the tree, and I ate it."*

Had Adam not eaten the fruit that GOD told him not to, that Eve told him to, that the snake told her to, everyone would still be in their rightful position, and that position is in the Garden of Eden.

The man responsible for everything was the CEO Adam. But when trouble came, he did not repent, and take responsibility, he blamed GOD (Genesis 3:12), which shows that Adam had also moved from his submission and gave up his position as leader.

Many believers (women) are understanding that submission is not a bad thing, it's actually a form of protection. And we are commanded to respect him (1 Peter 3:1) in his position just as David had to respect Saul. Ladies, we are not punks, or losing our independence, this was the order placed by God for our protection. And some things that we as married couples are not in agreement in, we rest in the responsibility with husband, because he is the head and has the final say; so, if it doesn't work so if it doesn't work, it's HIS FAULT. LOL

CHAPTER 7

HE WAS MARRIED

I've only been with one married man; that I know of. This guy, James, a music producer, flew me to Los Angeles to introduce me to some of the people he was connected to and give me a chance to see if Los Angeles is where I wanted to be. We stayed with his celebrity friend "Mike" who was going through a VERY messy divorce that required two bodyguards to stay in the home 24/7. I stayed in the room, in the bed with James but we had never had any type of intimacy.

Mike had two daughters who seemed to adore me and loved when I would "make their hair pretty." One weekend, the girls, five years old and seven years old, came back from spending the weekend with their mom, the youngest daughter looked at James and stated, "My mommy said that you are a married man and she, (pointing to me) is not your wife." Omg, how embarrassed and ashamed I was. A young child was able to call me out and understand that we were wrong. It was time to go for I knew those girls would never look at me the same and seemed to had lost respect for me.

That night, which was my last night after being there seven days, I laid in bed feeling ashamed of myself. James finally came into the room as usual but this time he stood there and stared at me. Silenced for about a minute, standing six feet four inches, dark chocolate skin with a milk dud looking bald head and said, "I want to make love to you." I looked at him strangely with no comment. After getting no response from me, he said, "I know what I'll do, I'm going to go make some music." I laid in bed, as usual, with my big t-shirt and gym shorts on. James came back about twenty minutes later and got into bed with me and began to take my shorts and panties down while kissing on the back of my neck while I laid on my side facing away from him. I knew where this was headed as my heart started beating hard, I began breathing faster, and my clitoris began to pulsate. His big strong hand slowly moved up and down my leg and thighs, as he kissed my neck. His lips were so soft and I did not stop him. After sliding my shorts and panties off my feet, we were still in the spoon position. He pulled the comforter back and kneeled down to the floor. As his right hand worked its' way up the middle of my legs, he reached my knees slowly parting them. He grabbed the right knee and pulled it away from the other, now I'm on my back and my legs are open. He slowly and gently began to kiss my inner thighs one after the other. That teaser was driving me crazy. Finally, he used his tongue with experience; he knew what he was doing. He was about 15 years my senior.

I could not completely let go but, I did not stop him. All the while all I could think about was, *this man is married, I'm going to hell, One day I'm going to regret this, 'You will reap what you sow,' OMG this will come back on me....* By this time, approximately two minutes, I felt the arch in my back and the volcano erupted.

Afterward, I never looked at him, I closed my legs and turned over feeling worse. Sensing it, he laid down and went to sleep.

I was up it seemed like forever. I could not believe what had just happened. I just couldn't stop my brain from the tornado of words: *He's married, and he won't leave his wife! What do you get from this? What if his wife finds out? This man has kids what if they find out? What if your name gets out? Will he look at you with the same friendship, He will not leave his wife. Adulterer! Cheater! No good! 'The other woman!' Side chick. Side piece. 'You will reap what you sow. You will reap what you sow.'*

And that I did, in my first marriage, first, I believe my first husband only married me to be able to have sex with me and, get more benefits for when he was ready to re-enter the army. Our marriage lasted less than one year. In four months, he would stay out late and have very very sexual and intimate conversations with other women. (One conversation got back to me, "...she can't suck D*#k good.") I remember this was the same complaint with the married guy used, "My wife doesn't do this, my wife doesn't do that."

Yes, I reaped what I sowed. I disrespected someone else's covenant and marriage, and my husband and other women disrespected ours.

CHAPTER 8

WE PUSHED EACH OTHER TO ANOTHER

Lucas and I were a popular couple with the Fraternity chapter that he was very active with and because was a poet. We'd go out to pretty much any place that had open mic. Before dating him, I didn't get out much so this was new and fun. He didn't drink, smoke, or cuss but he never opposed nor judged me for having a drink. In fact, he would buy because he'd never ever allowed me to spend my own money.

Many times, we'd be out and men would disrespect Lucas by approaching me, saying, or doing something on the sly. There were men who personally knew us, that would disrespect our relationship on social media. Well, Lucas came over one evening and asked me to stop entertaining these particular guys that openly disrespected our relationship on social media. I thought the flirting was harmless and entertaining, and I allowed it to continue, even after his multiple requests.

One day I received an inbox from a lady telling me that Lucas had cheated on me with her. Well, I don't believe women off the bat and I told her unless she comes with dates and times, don't contact me anymore. She sent messages with two dates and both hotels.

While reading these messages, I remembered recently, while visiting his mom she asked him, "Does she know that girl keeps calling me?" Lucas replied, "Nah mom, I'm just hoping she will finally give up." I didn't say a word in front of his mom but once we got in the car, I stated, "I heard what your mom said and you have not mentioned this to me at all. So, I don't want to hear anything about these guys anymore." That was his open door, that was his opportunity to fess up; but, he didn't.

After reading the messages, I called Lucas, "WHO IS THIS FUNNY LOOKING GIRL IN MY INBOX!" He swore against the allegations so strongly that I believed him and told her unless she has proof, DO NOT contact me anymore with this mess. About ten minutes later she sent phone records and screenshots of text messages with his phone number. I showed them to him and he strongly insisted that he had not seen nor spoken to her. NOW I'M CONFUSED. I didn't know whether to believe MY OWN eyes that showed PROOF that was in MY HAND, or my boyfriend.

To make a long story short, it took about a week for Lucas to admit to the **phone** stuff but STRONGLY denied, that he never "had sexual relations with that woman." But, a week was three days past my grace period because by day four I had already called both hotels, where I had to lie about who I was to get the information that I needed to get receipts faxed to me, emails from managers, I called other men to replay the whole scenario and give me their opinions, I found and had spoken with people who knew the girl and her character, I called phone company about phone records and how to know when how far back they can find records and archives. I found out what school she went to and spoke to a few of our mutual friends. I talked to other poets and had them to look up those dates to see if they had poetry night and where; I mean I was in full investigation and interview mode. It was crazy!

Not saying that Lucas was right in CHOOSING to entertain another woman but I had to know why. He knew I had been in a bad relationship before him. So WHY? This was an amazing guy who treated me as if God had put him to sleep and when he woke up I was there.

After speaking with a few guys, some helpful, some opportunist, I understood. Whether Lucas slept with her or not, my constant disregard for my man's feelings was, in fact, total disrespect. I realized that I had to take responsibility for my part in pushing him to another woman; BUT, he made a CHOICE.

Eventually, I forgave Lucas but the wound was too deep that I couldn't forget. I was devastated. Even though it hurt, I understood him entertaining another woman. Although I didn't like it, we could've gotten past it because I had a part in it, but the DIShonesty, the LIE- broke my heart.

He was a good man, but my love for him was not the same, and nothing he could do was able to change it. I could no longer trust his word.

What you won't do, another man will do.

Lucas and I continued our off again on-again relationship for about four years. He would not give up. His love for me and the way he treated me, kept calling me back by default. Lucas had set the bar so high that I had not come across another man who could reach it, until Hunter.

Hunter, who was shooting a short film and asked if I would be in it. Lucas was not too happy about how much time I was spending with Hunter but it was strictly business. Two years after Lucas and I had our first situation, I was hit with a very upsetting life situation. It was very traumatic and upsetting. The next night I had gotten more information, which caused more stress. Lucas had called and I immediately told him what happened and the new information I had just received. Lucas, began to question me about Hunter. That further infuriated me because I was having a moment and he was not attentive to my hurt. We began to argue and I hung up. And now that I'm thinking about Hunter, I called him to cry on his shoulder. Hunter came over and took me out to eat. We ate, had drinks, and talked. He was my shoulder to cry on.

Hunter, who was very respectful, made sure I got in the house safely; I invited him inside for a movie (No, this time I did not have a plan, as I spoke about in <u>The Divorce</u>.) We watched three movies and then I shocked him, and myself, by making a move on him.

Hunter and I dated for a year before his job moved him out of state; I chose not to go.

Survey says – WHAT MEN LIKE

"WE LIKE IT WHEN OUR WOMEN FLIRT WITH US."

"Men like reaction we don't like to read your minds."

"Public flirtation behind closed doors expectation. When we're in public I love when my wife grab my chest because she already know when we get behind closed doors it is on!"

"Don't say, we need to talk! Just address problem and say, 'Okay how we going to handle it??'"

"Unspoken communication - you can tell by they respond to the flirtation."

"The quickest way for a husband to lose passion for wife is when she stops believing in him or treats him with disrespect."

"It makes us want to do more when you all notice even the little things we do and compliment them."

CHAPTER 9

THE PERFECT MATE

When you speak about your spouse negatively you are actually doing a disservice to yourself. Actually you should be embarrassed because, **you chose to marry them**!

Proverbs 11:12 NLT It is foolish to belittle one's neighbor; a sensible person keeps quiet.

Proverbs 31:11 Her husband has full confidence in her and lacks nothing of value. 12She brings him good, not harm, all the days of her life.

You may say, well they weren't that way when I married them. Well, nine times out of ten, they were; you were in love/happy and you chose to ignore them or felt you could change them.

If she didn't cook or clean before then "I do" will not make. Not that it's a bad thing; especially if she works and brings home the bacon too. If he was lazy or a mama's boy, then after, "I do," lock you in, it does not get better.

Accept people, flaws and all. Remember the 80/20 rule is real because there is no perfect human so in the beginning, especially if you are 40+, you should've known that you didn't want a mate that smokes, or does not like oral sex.

Now if you have this mate and you have, for example, stopped smoking but they chose to continue, that is where you will have to take your mate to God. Just because you chose to stop doesn't automatically mean your mate should stop too. It would be nice tho.

If your mate doesn't like to clean, and you married them like that, and you have no children with chores, then you may want to buy paper ware, or budget a house keeper.

Don't make a big deal over what already was before you married them. And, "You knew I was like this before you married me" is not excuse for not wanting to do better.

"The grass is greener on the other side," because somebody, is putting in work.

Write down their 80% and focus on that while God work on the 20%.

THE DIVORCE

CHAPTER 48

"**I made the choice** to marry John with the waving **RED FLAGS** and the **FLASHING WARNING** signs. I did NOT ignore them.... I simply collected them believing I could work with them and make a difference and prove everybody wrong. I chose John out of my pain and current circumstances... I needed him; well, maybe not **him** but I needed the love, affirmation, and acceptance that he gave me. I'd always felt that I was never enough."

"...I owe him an apology for **unrealistic expectations**. I tried to make him be something he was not. I put him in a role and expected him to play it..."

WHERE TO FIND IT Biblehub.com (NLT)
(NIV)

✓ Oral Sex - <u>Hebrews 13:4</u> Give honor to marriage, and remain faithful to one another in marriage.

✓ No sex - <u>1 Corinthians 7:3</u> The husband should fulfill his marital duty to his wife, and likewise the wife to her husband.

✓ Extramarital, Threesome, Swinging - <u>1 Cor 6:9</u> Do you not know that the wicked will not inherit the kingdom of God? Do not be deceived: Neither the sexually immoral, nor idolaters, nor adulterers, nor men who submit to or perform homosexual acts

✓ Premarital / Recreational / Sex - <u>1 Cor 6:18</u> Flee from sexual immorality. All other sins a person commits are outside the body, but whoever sins sexually, sins against their own body. <u>Exodus 20:14</u>

✓ Adultery, Pornography? Strip Club? -
Commandment #6: <u>Exodus 20:14</u> You shall not commit adultery.

<u>Deut. 22:22</u> If a man is found lying with a married woman, then both of them shall die. <u>Colossians 3:5</u>, <u>Genesis 2:24</u>, <u>1 John 2:16</u>

✓ God Understands That The Flesh Is Weak & We Have Needs / I'm Not Perfect / We Are Human – <u>Matthew 7:22,23</u> 22Many will say to Me on that day, 'Lord, Lord, did we not prophesy in Your name, and in Your name drive out demons and perform many miracles?' 23Then I will tell them plainly, 'I never knew you; depart from Me, you workers of lawlessness.' <u>Proverbs 28:9</u>, <u>Phil. 3:13</u>

REPENT / FORGIVENESS

<u>Jer. 17:10</u> But I, the LORD, search all hearts and examine secret motives. I give all people their due rewards, according to what their actions deserve."

<u>1John 1:9</u>, <u>Amos 5:14</u>, <u>Hebrews 8:12</u>, <u>Hosea 14:4</u>

CHAPTER 10

A POWERFUL DRUG

It's been said that girls have sex with boys to get a **hug** after; boys **hug** girls to get sex after.

For women: Affection = Hug
For men: Hug = Sex

HUSBANDS: When your wife is having a bad day, grab her and hug her. Don't try to solve the problem yet. Let your hug be a warm embrace. Let her snuggle into your chest and feel you heartbeat. Make her feel safe, and covered. Don't try to have sex. Just be present.

WIVES: Lay your head on his chest. Hear his heartbeat. Feel his heartbeat. Allow him to hold you. It's okay to be vulnerable. It's okay; allow him to be your strength.

Vice Versa

WIVES: When your husband comes in from a bad day, possibly beaten by the world, and life, just represent Peace. Walk him to the couch and hand him a drink, get on your knees, and get to massage his feet or shoulders; or, if you're exhausted, sit on the couch with your back against the arm, put one leg up on the couch, inviting him in to come, sit, and lie back on you. Now that you're in the, "I got you" position, put your arms around him and embrace him; gently rub his arms, chest, and stomach. While your king is puddy in your hands, make the offer, "Do you want to talk about it?" If he says No, then do not take it personal. Just give him peace. This could possibly end up in sex; but, either way, he's relaxed. Mission Accomplished.

HUSBANDS: It's okay to not be so much MACHO. She will appreciate you allowing her to have your back. Just relax. WARNING: We (women) like it when you communicate; if you talk about what's wrong, during this tender moment. So, nine times out of ten, she's about to initiate.

Hug – an oxytocin releaser ☺

THE FLAME

- What is LOVE - <u>1 Cor 13:4</u>
  4 Love is patient, love is kind. It does not envy, it does not boast, it is not proud. 5 It does not dishonor others, it is not self-seeking, it is not easily angered, it keeps no record of wrongs. 6 Love does not delight in evil but rejoices with the truth. 7 It always protects, always trusts, always hopes, always perseveres.
  8 Love never fails

- God calls marriage "Good." - According to <u>Genesis 2:22-24</u> 22 The LORD God fashioned into a woman the rib which He had taken from the man, and brought her to the man. 23 <u>The man said, "This is now bone of my bones, And flesh of my flesh; She shall be called Woman, Because she was taken out of Man."</u> 24 For this reason a man shall leave his father and his mother, and be joined to his wife; and they shall become one flesh

- Anger - <u>Ephesians 4:26</u> NIV In your anger do not sin": Do not let the sun go down while you are still angry

- With God all things are possible - <u>Matthew 19:26 NIV</u> Jesus looked at them and said, "With man this is impossible, but with God all things are possible."

- Stand still and see the salvation – <u>2 Chronicles 20:17 NLT</u> But you will not even need to fight. Take your positions; then stand still and watch the LORD's victory. He is with you

- Spouse won by mates conduct – 1Cor 7:16, 1Pet 3:1

<u>1 Cor 7:16, 17</u> 15But if the unbeliever leaves, let him go. The believing brother or sister is not bound in such cases. God has called you to live in peace. 16How do you know, wife, whether you will save your husband? Or how do you know, husband, whether you will save your wife? 17Regardless, each one should lead the life that the Lord has assigned to him and to which God has called him. This is what I prescribe in all the churches.

Good movies to watch: <u>Fireproof</u> and <u>War Room</u>.

CHAPTER 11

OVULATION "HOT"

I remember when my Chihuahua had starting having periods. During this time she would become very aggressive towards the kids and myself. The way I found out she was in heat was when she braced her legs tightly around my arm and began to thrust back and forth with force. I thought, *What the heck is she doing to my arm???* I had seen boy dogs do this but never a girl dog. Another time she was so aggressive, she scratched my arm up. This was in addition to a swollen vulva and spots of blood that dripped from it. Ugh!

I remember a time I had a beautiful dog named Puntin. I had to call the Dog Pound because there were about eight dogs in our backyard, but what I wasn't expecting was for them to take my dog too; and, fined us for not having our dog spayed. I don't remember verbatim what the fine read but I know it had something to do with "Inciting a riot." Yes, because my dog was not spayed, her ovulation scent (pheromones) was calling all the boys to the yard.

Well what I found is when a female is ovulating or in heat, any type of female, female dog, female elephant, her body prepares to produce and give life therefore, it craves sperm. Her body is wanting to mate, which was designed by

our Creator. (Genesis 1:28 – "Be fruitful and multiply.")
Which is another reason she can become a slippery slope.

Wife of 4 years and mother of two
Wife, 33, 4'11 "My husband is 6ft. I wouldn't mind trying something new but I get nervous because it's foreign I am willing and trainable. I want him to teach me. He can say, "Let's try this."

CHAPTER 12

THE REAL

Husbands, there are wives who "fake it." Some, not all. Why? Because she doesn't want to hurt your feelings. Women, when we do this, we are cheating him, and ourselves. If your husband loves you, he should desire to pleasure you. Husbands, I'm going to let you in on a little secret, you (men) can tell when a woman is faking it; BUT, You must not be a selfish lover to know this. You have to be in tuned to your wifes' body.

If you are performing oral and you are using your fingers during your performance (tickling her G-spot), when she reaches an orgasm, not only does her body: legs, thighs, toes, and/or etc. began to vibrate, but the inside of her vagina may began to contract. Pretty much everything below the belly button and thigh region should react. Many times a woman is unable to speak. Her heart is racing, her back bone is arched and she's tense.

This relates to ONLY some women, NOT ALL. And, this is where communication comes to play because, not ALL women have the same reaction. Some have noticeably physical reactions, and others have neurological reactions. Again, HUSBANDS, get to know your wife. WOMEN, get to know, and understand, your vagina.

CHAPTER 13

BE TRAINABLE

Husbands, wives, allow your mate to coach you. TRUST ME you will be much happier later. I remember a relationship where I told a guy what I liked or I needed to get to the orgasm, "Move up, make your mouth wetter, use your fingers, etc." Well, he hated it and finally he couldn't take it any longer. He actually told me, "Don't tell me what to do."

"Huh?" I asked.

He responded, "I don't like when you tell me what to do. Just let me figure it out."

I laid there completely turned off. Staring at the ceiling. *This is disgusting,* I thought. Not only am I not being pleasured, but this dude is actually just down there trying to follow a map when I am the GPS. *How long is this going to take?*

As I mentioned before, "I was devastated when I got word that my first husband told a girl, "She don't suck d*ck good." OMG, he was my husband. REALLY??? I would've thought he'd be glad that his wife wasn't a professional Head nurse but I could be his intern waiting for training.

THE COVENANT / VOWS / PROMISE

Genesis 2:23 The man said, "This is now bone of my bones, And flesh of my flesh; She shall be called Woman, Because she was taken out of Man." **24**For this reason a man shall leave his father and his mother, and be joined to his wife; and they shall become one flesh.**25**And the man and his wife were both naked and were not ashamed.

I _____ take you _____
To be my lawful wedded husband/wife
To have and to hold from this day forward
For better or for worse
For richer or for poorer
In sickness and in health
Til death do us part
According to God's Holy Ordinance
In the presence of God, I make this vow.

Officiant: Do you **promise** to Love, Honor, Protect, Forsaking all others...

Groom: I do

Officiant: Do you **promise** to Love, Honor, Obey, Forsaking all others...

Bride: I do

"You shall be careful to perform what goes out from your lips, just as you have voluntarily vowed to the Lord you God what you have promised." Jesus said that "every careless word that men shall speak, they shall render account for it in the day of judgment" (Matt 12:36).

THE BREACH / DIVORCE / DI-VISION /

"FOR I HATE DIVORCE," says the LORD, the God of Israel.
Malachi 2:16 NLT

Many has made those promises **UNTIL**:

- ✓ **Sickness** came
- ✓ **Riches** came
- ✓ **Poor** came
- ✓ **Health** came (spouse, children had recovered from i.e. cancer, surgery, etc. Or even while the spouses were healthy but just waited until the children had gotten older. A spouse has gotten on their feet and they, themselves, left.)

Until it was time to walk through those promises.

Biblical Reasons Divorce Is Allowed:

Repentance and Forgiveness is God; Divorce is last resort.

❖ **Sexual Immorality**
  ➢ Matthew 5:32 NLT But I say that a man who divorces his wife, unless she has been unfaithful, causes her to commit adultery. And anyone who marries a divorced woman also commits adultery.

❖ **Abandonment**
  ➢ 1 Corinthians 7:15 NLT But if the husband or wife who isn't a believer insists on leaving, let them go. In such cases the Christian husband or wife is no longer bound to the other, for God has called you to **live in peace** (physical abuse).

❖ **Physical Abuse**
  ➢ 1 Corinthians 6:19 NLT Don't you know realize that your body is the temple of the Holy Spirit, who lives in you and was given to you by GOD? You do not belong to yourself for you were bought with a high price. So you must Honor GOD with your body.
  ➢ Ephesians 5:28 NLT ...husbands ought to love their wives as they love their OWN bodies.

- ▪ <u>1 John 3:15</u> NLT Anyone who hates another brother or sister is really a murderer at heart. And you know that murderers don't have eternal life within them.
- ➤ <u>Colossians 3:19 NLT</u> Husbands, love your wives and do not be harsh with them.
- ➤ <u>Deuteronomy 30:19 NLT</u> Today I have given you the choice between life and death, between blessings and curses. Now I call on heaven and earth to witness the choice you make. Oh, that you would choose life, so that you and your descendants might live!
- ➤ <u>1 Peter 3:7 NLT</u> ...you husbands must give honor to your wives. Treat your wife with understanding as you live together. She may be weaker than you are but she is your equal partner in GOD'S GIFT of new life. Treat Her As You Should So Your Prayers Will Not Be Hindered.
- ➤ <u>Romans 13: 2 NLT</u> So anyone who rebels against authority is rebelling against what GOD instituted, and they will be punished.
  - ▪ Domestic abuse and child abuse are crimes against the law.

<u>The National Domestic Hotline</u> **1-800-799-7233**

CHAPTER 14

SPONTANEOUS-NESS

Be spontaneous! That stuff is FUN!!! I don't care how old you are, or how old your marriage is, SPONTANEOUS-NESS never gets old. Anyone would like a surprise every now and then. Being spontaneous does not have to be expensive, it can be a simple picnic at the park, or picnic in the Livingroom. If you have children, it can be taking the kids over to a friends' house or have a trustworthy teen who likes mall or skating rink money, or with girls, you can have their hair done. Teens are the cheapest sitters, but they have to be responsible and reliable. Guys, well again, responsible, if your child has an Xbox, that's good. Guys like games or just mall money as well.

(Again, one thing we have to be mindful, there is a such thing as **Molestation. It can be done by Male or Female, to a Male or Female.** Young or old, you cannot tell a Molester by just looking at them so it'd be a great idea to keep a phone, hidden camera, and especially talking to your children about NO means NO). You may not reach the predator but you can reach your child before the predator reaches them.)

Spontaneous, do something that will create a memory, "Remember that time we did... I wonder if someone heard us… What if someone had seen us?" **I AM NOT SUGGESTING TO DO ANYTHING ILLEGAL OR COMMIT A CRIME.** I'm saying create that "remember the time" or night to remember event. Find that friend that you all are cool with and pull a <u>Boomerang</u> scene in the bathroom. "BANG, BANG, BANG." Do not disrespect your friends home be sure to communicate first. Go to the garage, ditch the party!

There was a couple who were going through postpartum depression. "Man, when I came in and saw my wife had her hair done and put a part on the side instead of in the middle like she normally do, it was different, that was SEXY!"

That little bit, something as simple changing where she parted her hair, he noticed it, and found it sexy.

And let the men of the church say...

Spontaneity, does not have to cost money. "One day my husband came in from work and when he walked through the door I had taped my nipples to erect. I had nothing but a t-shirt on so that the first thing he saw were the high beams." – J. L. Divorced mom of 4, 59 years old

"I went to my husbands' job around his lunch time. When they called him down, I had on a big coat. When he walked me back to my car, I flashed him. I laughed all the way home. Boy was he ready!" - S. Diane 68 year old mother of 2, married 39 years

.

Chapter 15

Give HEAD before bed

"Get in her head through the day, she'll get on your head at night." Tori Lynn

Husbands, if you make love to her mind during the day, she'll make love to your body at night, and, there's a strong possibility that she'll initiate! VERY STRONG. For the average woman, sex is mental. WE LOVE SEX JUST AS MUCH AS MEN but our minds have to be relaxed.

Men have to get hard, women have to get soft (our minds).

Wives minds are constantly thinking, *"What am I going to cook, What will I wear to work tomorrow, I need to iron, Am I going to be late picking up the kids, traffic, Daycare expenses, competition at the work place, I need a raise, I HATE MY JOB, husband thinks I'm nagging, why isn't he helping, am I a good wife, am I anywhere near the Proverbs 31 Woman, how do I get my point across w/o a fight, baby is sick, etc."* That list is doubles when the husband is lazy because she has to think and do things that he doesn't think to do. 1 Corinthians 7:34 NLT – But a married woman has to care for her earthly responsibilities and how to please her husband.

Husband, when was the last time you asked your wife, "Are you happy with me?" or, "What can I do to make your life better?" Don't assume that because she does everything without complaining, that she doesn't need help or that she's happy.

Wives, husbands are not mind readers! State the problem or ask for what you need, in simple sentences. Try to cut out the extra because men like to solve problems, once they know what it is. If you don't communicate, it's possible that you will end up resenting him for not tending to your needs. (If you married a lazy man, you are going to need much help and prayer. Especially for yourself.)

Husbands, you must also communicate! WE LOVE IT WHEN YOU COMMUNICATE!!! Don't assume your wife is "trippin," doesn't find you sexy, or that she's not fun anymore. Ask her questions! Ask her what you can do to make her load a little lighter. Better yet, don't ask, ACT!!! Get caught working: cook, vacuum, help kids with homework, cut the grass, etc. Get into her mind & find out what will make your wife feel special. Go above & beyond. IT RECIPROCATES. If you take care of her through the day, nine times out of ten she will take care of you at night. . The Bible says, "Don't let the sun go down on your anger."

Wives, Go Head (pun intended).

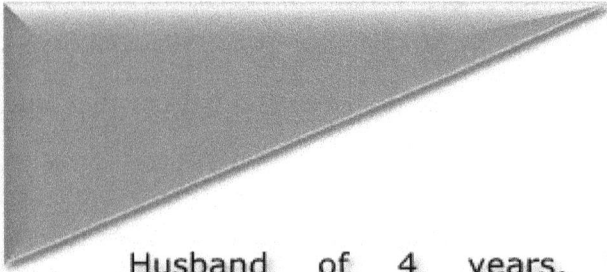

Husband of 4 years, "I remember complimenting my wife; because I have a beautiful wife, but at one point I stopped telling her because one time I said, 'Baby, you are so beautiful' and she said, 'I know.'"

Tori, "Well, was she playing or serious?"

Husband of 4 years, "It didn't matter, all she had to do was say, 'Thank you. So, I stopped complimenting her.

"When she's non-receptive I back off. I may get in my feelings. I would like her to show interests. Flirt back." Married man 4 years, two children

CHAPTER 16

HAS YOUR LIFE GOTTEN BETTER, SINCE I'VE BEEN IN IT???

There could never be another Dr. Martin Luther King. Coretta Scott King would've had to settle for a good man because, even with flaws and all, Dr. Martin Luther King was a GREAT man. There will never be another President Barak Obama or First Lady Michelle Obama. The both of them, even without each other, are irreplaceable. (And, their infectious love and affection for each other; they're irreplaceable.) There will never be another Mother Theresa, Princess Diana and so on.

Of course, many of us know about the 80/20 rule so that 80% has to be so on point that the 20% is covered with the shadow of the 80% and clothed with 1 Corinthian 3:4-7.

As with Tyler Perry's stage play, "Madea's Family Reunion," the girl asked her fiancé, "What do I do for you?" If you ask your mate that question and they don't know what you're talking about, you're in trouble. At your job, are they interviewing people to fill your position? If there was a lay-off, could you be the first person they let go or have you made it to where they just can't fire you, they have to find another spot for you in the company, or you would be the last to go only because they've tried everything else.

Make it wear you're NEEDED!!! It's one thing to feel

> ## *Why do I need her/him?*
> ## *Why does he/she need me?*

wanted but to feel <u>needed</u> is amazing.

There is never a time when a women needs you more is when there's some type of trauma or new baby. She needs your strength. Of course she can do it alone (as I did), but I would have loved my husband to simply fix me a sandwich, take turns waking up with the baby at night, let me steal a nap, massage my back and or feet, make grocery store runs, attend Dr's appointments, carrying baby carrier, tending to house or other children, and did I mention, SLEEP. I needed him during that time. However, everything was done without him. He taught me that he WAS NOT needed.

Many affairs are born at this time because, "no sex for six weeks", waking up every two hours, weight gain, the wish for weight loss, stress, post-partum depression, disconnect, regret, shame, attitude, etc. For some women, this season draws them closer to her husband more than ever before.

If your past child bearing stage, another reason a woman can need you is while she carries the weight of the empty nest syndrome. Again, at this stage, a woman may no longer feel needed if she has no other way to fill her time after no longer being a teacher, soccer mom, chauffeur, crisis negotiator, funder, etc. she will need you. When the last child goes, she needs a new norm, a new spice. Lucky for you, you will be there to help her through. What are some ways to help her reinvent?

Today, women are taught to be independent. Black women have been taught to be independent from slavery. Actually, it was a learned behavior. When slaves were married, the master would separate the unity by placing the wife and children on Plantation A, and the husband on Plantation B or he was sold to a different master. The "Willie Lynch" stamped it, and it became part of the African-American cultural, for years to come. Black families have not UNLEARNED this teaching.

Unfortunately, many cultures are okay with being divided. Divorces are at an all-time high. Why? Well besides, finances and communication, people don't feel needed because people are becoming more self-centered and self-sufficient.

My grandparents had been married for fifty-two years. But, on February 7, my 84 year old grandmother passed away; then, seven months later, my grandfather joined her. He was not ill and he had convinced us that he was going to live to the age of 100. But, she was his reason for living. He was her hero with even the small things. She depended on him to have dinner, ice cream, and simply his presence. In my heart, I believe the reason my 94 year old full-of-life grandfather passed away was, he no longer felt needed.

SURVEY – WOMEN
The best part of Making Love

The #1 answer:
"It's the connection, the oneness"
"I like the reaction/sounds."

"I aim to please. I know it's going to make him happy."

"I like sex, a lot! Many times it's not about him. I want it so much that sometimes it creates a problem. He'll say, 'You are killing me.'"

"I like to pull b*#@ch card. I get off on reactions. I cannot stand a silent man. Let me know if you like what I'm doing or don't. If you don't give me some type of reaction, I will think you are not being pleased and I will get up."

"Tori, I have stopped and got up in the middle of sex because I got bored with his silence."

"I like it when he climaxes. The face, the tensing up, the grunts."

"I like it when he talks dirty. But, I don't when he talks so much that it breaks my concentration."

SURVEY – MEN
Feelings about sex and oral

These answers are from 10 men all over the age of forty. In a Nut shell (pun), they pretty much all gave the same answers...

The #1 answers:
"It's more mental now." "It's about the connection."

"She trusts me enough to do it."

"I like when she gets off; it's a turn on knowing she's turned on."

"I like that she wants to please me."

"I like to watch her face. When she bite her lip. Or how she looks at me when I'm inside of her."

"Sometimes I'm turned on just by the moans sounds still in my head."

"I like the rhythm of it when she moves her body. It's like being on a dance floor."

"I like the dominant feeling. The submissive thing. Kind of like a roll play. Making a man feel in charge."

With these answers, and it seems at this age, men are not just all about sex anymore. The myth that, "All men just want sex..." seems to be changing.

CHAPTER 17

THE LOVE POTION

A major turn off for sex is a bad smell. Women have a natural vaginal scent, many of us don't like, but men are crazy about it. A whiff of the vaginal smell is such a turn on for men they can erect just from the scent alone. So ladies, let's embrace it. As long as it's not a foul, musty, or fishy smell, our vagina's natural scent is great. It's God-given. It's natural. Studies even show that the scent of the Vagina is an aphrodisiac.

Not many people like the outdoor yard sweaty smell; and, it can be a MAJOR turn off if someone is in the pubic area. (Now there are some sweat smells that can be a turn on for some women so know your mate.) You want to stay as dry and fresh as possible. Here some ways:

- SEXUAL TRANSMITTED DISEASE FREE
- REGULAR BATHS/SHOWERS
- Body butters and more by Tori Lynn (for men and women)
- TABOO PASSION POTION edible massage body butter (Chocolate / Vanilla) by Tori Lynn
- Cotton underwear
- Vagina Steam

- Deodorant in inner thighs
- Perfume spray or oil between the thighs
- Bathing in Epsom Salt or Baking Soda
- Wet wipes
- Groomed garden. Not that you have to be bald but hair holds moisture; too much moisture, for too long, usually began to smell like mildew or musty. Keep it groomed. Ladies, keep the secret garden, a secret. Don't let the KitKat smell like a kit-and-caPoodle.

I'm sure there are more but the list above is either already in our homes and/or easily accessible.

Ladies, be careful with products having direct contact with your vagina (unless it's been clinically tested and approved). You don't want to wake up one morning with that Oochie Coochie.

Also, sex. If you are into freaky stuff and want to put things into your vagina, get ready for the Oochie Coochie. Yes, even a peanut-buttered penis (Anal to Vaginal) and dirty fingers can put that kitty on blaze. Use your best judgment.

As Kool Moe Dee would say, "Three days later, go see the Drrrrrrrrr."

Just try to avoid putting anything in the vagina altogether unless it's "made" for the vagina i.e.: penis, tampons, and condoms (you may be allergic to condoms).

If you know you are highly allergic to this or that, DO NOT USE IT!!!

Also, it's not safe to use Coconut oil with condoms. You may wake up pregnant; or worse, with an "OOCHIE" in that Coochie.

QandA

Question: What's something that your husband does or can do to put you in the mood?

Answer: (Average answer) Helping out more around the house. It's a turn on when he helps with the kids or help out around the house.

Chapter 18

DON'T KNOCK IT TIL YOU TRY IT

"What you won't do..."

Spouses, if you want to introduce your mate to something new, and if they trust you, usually they may be willing to try anything at least once. Be SURE they're stress-free and **relaxed**. For example oral, toys, or sex somewhere daring etc., if you would like to try this with your mate, especially if they're African American:

- You will really have to work on your wife emotionally. She will definitely have to trust you first and foremost.
- It'd be a good idea to communicate the **importance** of your feelings/why you want to do this or why you want your mate to perform this.
- If he or she is willing to try, you will need LOTS and LOTS of lube. There's nothing like the pain of carpet burn, and it's sure to be a turn-off.

PAY ATTENTION: If he or she doesn't seem to really be "feeling it", even if you haven't gotten far, then stop. You don't want your mate to feel forced, nor do you want to make them uncomfortable. This will allow them to trust you and they MAY be willing to try it again OR will be willing to try something else. DON'T FORCE IT. It just may NOT be their thing, at least not right now, and that's okay. **You definitely**

want to appreciate him or her for trying it. If for some reason they are not willing to try the act for you, that's your mate; respect their decision. DO NOT APPEAR ANGRY OR RESENTFUL and definitely do not try manipulation, **"What you won't do, someone else will."** That's a NO, NO! Again many people have been raised that sex is nasty and is good for only making babies. Give them time to consider something foreign or new. Also, this will be your opportunity to see if she'd be willing to try something else. Even something as little as role play or sex in odd places, like the car. If you are the unwilling mate this is where you give-and-take, meet halfway, or compromise, "I won't do anal sex because there are health risks involved, I don't want my hole to become loose, or... but I'm willing to try..." This is your opportunity to explore together.

WARNING: DO NOT EXPECT YOUR WIFE / HUSBAND TO RESPOND AS A PAST FLING or EX RESPONDED EXPLORE YOUR MATE.

Mates don't set your spouse up, especially if he/she is a Believer. Don't use them to have a reason to <u>choose</u> to cheat.

Cheating is a **CHOICE.**

CHAPTER 19

TREASURE ISLAND

"If you get in her head through the day, she'll come for your head at night." Tori

Husbands, first set the mental mood. Here are some things that can be turn-ons with your twist to it. Starting with Q and A's from a few women, let's get started...

(WARNING: If your wife is African American and has a weave or fresh hairstyle, DO NOT TOUCH IT, you will turn her off with even the slightest graze of her hair and/or hairstyle. You can instantly kill the switch if she has to stop to go and look at or fix her hair.)

1. Flirt with her: send her text messages, wink at her, call her just because, schedule and pay for her to have a massage, or mani/pedi, pay one of HER bills, take her out to lunch, have her favorite flower delivered come through the door with them and etc.

2. **TAKE CHARGE!!!!**
   Make decisions, be creative, plan something, get kids situated, take initiative to cook, pick-up take-out, put children down for bed early or take them to sitter. Make it where she has no choice but to relax. Be the man and Take Charge!!!

3. SENSUALITY

Hopefully you've taken care of majority of her stresses. If she is relaxed, she should be melting like butter in your hands. Your touch is everything. Your touch alone should be erotic. She should be able to feel your passion for her even through your very finger tips. Lead with your hands as if you were leading on a dance floor. Again, take leadership with your hands. Use your <u>God-given</u> <u>male strength</u> but stay passionate. At this moment, you have permission to be in total control, TAKE IT!

4. The DISCOVERY ZONE

Pay attention to her body language. You can tell when she began to relax, her breathing should slow down; but, if or when she's aroused her breathing changes to faster, heavier, and deeper and her heart beats harder. If you kiss/lick on her ear, pay attention if she seems tickled or turned off, same as any other part of her body. Discover her safe zones and stay away from the war zones. Her nipples should now be tight at this point (Some women lose a little feeling in their nipples after children so you may have to be little rough for more feeling.) Nibble on her nipple with your tongue and teeth, give love bites. (Love bites should not be painful.) Remember: pay attention to how she responds. <u>Some women won't say anything because</u>

she doesn't want to hurt your feelings or hope you will hurry and pass that point.

5. Suck/Nibble on her bottom lip with tease. Don't just stick your tongue down her throat and definitely make sure your lips aren't crusty. Tease her with your tongue.

6. Hold the small of her back very close to you, as if you're holding a football (please, breath mint!) Bracing a woman close to your heart is captivating.

7. If you are standing behind her, kiss the back of her neck softly while you have her braced against you with your hand, widened, between the hip and the thigh. Let her feel your arousal. It's a turn on.

8. Massages!!! YESSSS, with strong hands!

9. AGAIN, be in tuned to your wife. Pay attention or ask her in a low sexy voice, "Do you like that?" If she doesn't give you a good reaction, or a sexy response, then move on.

10. FOREPLAY: By this time, you should have moved south. Play with her navel with your tongue. (If she doesn't like it, keep moving south.

11. Now, she should be completely, aroused and excited. You are face to face with Kitty. Your lips are just as important as your tongue. Do you remember where your hands were placed while riding a bike? Your hands should have her legs spread with fingers up top

and thumbs close in the inner thigh working, massaging, and caressing. Use your tongue to part her Kitty lips. (**MAKE SURE YOUR MOUTH IS WET!!! If your mouth is not wet enough, it will feel like semi-wet carpet and that is NOT pleasurable. Tolerable but not pleasurable. In fact, depending on how sensitive the clitoris is, it can be downright painful and a total turnoff. If she tolerates it, it's because she is hoping it will get better as she concentrates on *HURRY, ORGASM, HURRY!*)** While using your wet tongue, began to tease her by tongue kissing the clitoris.

Your wife should be reacting: Moans, squirms, spasms, faster breaths, and/or etc. If you are not, back off of it and began to play with her G-spot. (Reset) Her body should be responding, by now, by secreting fluid within. If for any reason, (there are many) she is not secreting little to no vaginal fluid, **KEEP SOME TYPE OF LUBRICATION READY**. If you don't have any, you will NEED LOTS of saliva, slobber, spit, drool, or whatever you want to call it, you will need it. A dry tongue is rough and uncomfortable. The more slippery your tongue and fingers are, the better. As I stated with the tongue, the finger(s) has to be slippery as well. It can hurt if it's not. Many times some sort of fluid will even cause the body to secrete even more.

(Ladies, be hydrated.) Husbands, take control! Don't be scared of Kitty. "Fake it until you make it."

TIP 1: ICE CREAM

Use your mouth AND lips as if you are eating your favorite ice cream out of a small bowl with no spoon. Your whole mouth is involved, licking, sucking, slurping, chasing, cleaning, etc.

TIP 2: APPLE SEEDS

 If you were to cut an apple in half, how would you suck out the seeds?

TIP 3: HAPPY BIRTHDAY

Sing Happy Birthday using your lips and tongue. NO VOICE!

WARNING: Unless it's <u>her</u> birthday, **<u>DO NOT</u>** sing Happy Birthday to her. She will kick you out for having her birthday mixed up with someone else's!

By now, your wife should be going crazy. She should be as tense as a shaken Coca-Cola bottle with the lid tight or bottle of champagne. You feel her body tensed and warm as the blood has swollen her clitoris. If her volcano is ready to explode, "cum," do not attempt to pull a trick and don't move off that spot. Whatever you were doing obviously worked. (One false move will cause her body to reset, and you will have to start back at number one.

That's if she's not disgusted, ready to move on, or turned off all together.) If your wife is taking a long time to have an orgasm "cum," she may need Direct Stimulation:

> **TIP:** Have you ever watched a dog attack anything: a sock, toys, pants leg, then you see the dog doesn't just attack with its' lips and tongue, its' entire face, and head is involved in the attack.

ADDED STIMULATION: YES, I'm talking about the **G-SPOT.** Alright for added stimulation, or when you are ready for the volcano to erupt, while you are licking, slurping, tonguing, and attacking the clitoris, insert one or two fingers inside her vagina one-fourth of the way up (1 to 2 inches in) and turn your fingers to the roof as if to say, "Come here Kitty Kitty." There you will find small rough spot just on the other side of her clitoris. Tickle or massage her G-spot while you're "eating her out." Now get ready for an insane involuntary muscle twitch spasm arched-backed soul leaving orgasm. You can still make her cum without using the G-spot but if you add the G, you are going to drive her insane and the Orgasm will be screaming and intense inside out. There are 8,000 nerve endings in the clitoris so here's your opportunity to blow her mind, body, and soul.

Again, every woman is different. Not all react the same way.

CAUTION: SLIPPERY WHEN WET

Now, that you have given your wife a **<u>clitoral</u>** orgasm, now make her have a **<u>vaginal</u>** orgasm. If her body did not produce much fluid, lube your tool and insert the head of your penis into her vagina about one to two inches in. (IF YOU ARE WELL ENDOWED, **DO NOT** INSERT ALL THE WAY IN FOR YOU WILL PASS THE G-SPOT!!!) Let the head of your penis massage her g-spot. It should NOT take long to cum again for she is already aroused, wet, and sensitive. 5,4,3,2, and POW!!!

WARNING: THESE ARE BASIC TIPS; HOWEVER, EVERY WOMAN IS DIFFERENT THAT'S WHY YOU HAVE TO EXPLORE AND DISCOVER WHAT WORKS. BUT BE PATIENT FOR YOUR "DIAGNOSIS" BECAUSE EITHER WAY THIS EXAMINATION SHOULD BE FUN FOR THE BOTH OF YOU.

Okay, play with this too!

I know you are aroused and excited by now but there's one more thing, now that you're ready to go all in. Insert your penis into her vagina and use your pelvic or pubic area to rub against her clitoris. Don't pounce on her, more thrust. Thrusting also allows you to have very close contact with her body which is very sensual.

.

**Things that should
LIVE by the bed**:

- Bottled waters for the throat

- Lubrication for the kitty

- Wet wipes for the genital cleanup

- Towel for the wet spot(s).

Alright ladies, I polled the men "What would you like more from your wife? The results are:

1. INIATE SEX!
2. "TAKE IT!"
3. BE SPONTANEOUS!

CHAPTER 20

SLIDING DOWN SLIPPERY SLOPE!

Being clear: "Take it" means to be spontaneous, suddenly, and not asking for his body. (Some used the term rape just to help describe what "take it" mean.)

Let's jump right in...

There's a saying, "The quickest way to a man's heart is through his stomach."

While your man is gone, get everything together for ShowTime. Create an environment of **peace**, (if you have children and can't get a sitter i.e.: get the kids out of your bedroom and demand that hour or two for yourselves.) Set your living room, or any room, up as you would an outdoor picnic. Have Lavender and/or Vanilla aromatherapy, or candles in the dim room. Have soft music, wine or his favorite drink ready for him, have your Nicety Girl outfit (under an outfit or dress), his favorite scent that he likes to smell on you, and have your husband's favorite meal cooked.

While he is eating, get him to talk about something, anything; if not, just flirt with him. Feed him, suck the gravy, juice, or wine off his bottom lip all while giving him eye contact.

While he's finishing his meal, be close enough to where he can see you but far enough where he can't touch you, began to slowly undress. Enjoy yourself undressing in front of him i.e.:

lick your lips, slowly rub your skin while looking at you him (you should look enticing). Now you should be dressed in your naughty Nighty.

If he's sitting on the floor, use your cat eyes as you get down on your knees and crawl to him (careful not to get carpet burned), and sit on top of him in cowgirl position. Dip his finger in the sauce, gravy, or your drink, and taste and lick it off using your tongue then close your lips and pull away from his finger and make the "Mmmmh" sound.

Grab the back of his head and tongue kiss him passionately. Unbutton his shirt or slip it over his head while delivering slow kisses to his neck. Be sure your lips are moist. Continue to seduce your husband. Kiss his earlobes (I know touching a man's ears with your mouth may sound disgusting; but, they like it so continue). Began kissing him from his and work your way down to his ears, to his neck. Ok stop and go school girl and give the little sucks (hickeys). Move down to his chest. Work your wet tongue around his man nipple as you force him to lie back. Now work the other man nipple. Watch his reaction because sometimes, one man nipple can be more sensitive to the other but work your tongue, lips, and mouth together as you lick, suck and give love-bites to it. Move back up and get a little more tongue as you let him know that you are enjoying yourself, as much as you are enjoying seducing him.

While kissing your husband, began to unzip his pants and keep kissing him as you move down to remove them. Go back to his chest and rotate kissing the man-nipples and belly button as you use your fingertips to graze his buttocks as you remove his underwear.

Now your husband should be naked. **Remember: KEEP YOUR MOUTH AND LIPS MOIST AT ALL TIMES.** Rotate between his lips, forehead, ears lobes, man nipples, and belly button so kiss, suck and bite then rotate, then move down; Kiss, suck, and bite then rotate then move down. Do this all the way down until you find the pubic bone.

Hopefully, your husband's chia pet is well-groomed. (If it's not, 9 times out of 10, he will let you mow that lawn but, do it another day if you can stand it). Mr. Lollipop should be turned on.

LOLLIPOP

*Remember, I'm only going over the basics.

1. Okay, grab your husbands' penis/"Lollipop" and hold it in your hand while you use your tongue to massage his navel, which creates great anticipation.

2. Grab the lollipop just as if you were getting ready to speak into a microphone. (Just as our main sensitivity is in the clitoris, the man's main sensitivity is in the head, marbles, and behind the sacks.) Get your mouth as wet as possible. With your hand holding the shaft of the

penis, place your mouth on the tip of the head and slowly glide down. PAUSE. Make sure you are comfortable as you do not want kill the mood by gagging, choking, nor vomiting (unless you want to; freak).

(Do not focus on "taking it all in" or "balls and all" just yet. Your husband is just happy that you are playing with his "balls and all." *Handle with care!*)

3. Okay, now the lollipop should be in your wet mouth, and your hand should be holding its' shaft. Passionately stroke his lollipop by moving your hand up and down in a slow rhythmic motion (jack him off). While doing this, let your wet lips stroke the head and let your tongue move as if you are licking a melting Popsicle and bob your head up and down at the same time.

TIP: FAKE IT TIL YOU MAKE IT. You may not feel comfortable because maybe you don't have much experience, or you may feel as if "I don't know what I'm doing!" No, a good husband will understand and be appreciative. Many of them know that we were raised in the church and were taught oral sex would put you in hell but remember the bible verse (Hebrews 13:4). Enjoy the experimentation. Watching his reaction should be enjoyable on its' own, and sometimes it can even be comical. Be trainable and Have FUN!

4. Take the lollipop out of your mouth and, as you would a melting Popsicle, lick around it and down the sides.

Place lollipop back in your mouth, place both hands, and a few fingers from both hands, and gently massage the shaft, with a little pressure, while moving your hands and mouth up and down, and add suction.

TIP: Every now and then, while the lollipop is in your mouth, LOOK UP AT HIM! "We (men) like it."

5. ADDED STIMULATION: continue #5 but take one hand down to the scrotum, "kiwis," place them in your hand, as you would two golf balls, and gently juggle them. Every now and then, put one in your mouth and tongue massage it and add suction, then do the other.

6. Go back to step #4 but this time, with your wet mouth on the head of the lollipop and move your head in a clockwise motion. You should feel the head on your tongue and the roof of your mouth.

TIP: NEVER EVER EVER, USE YOUR TEETH. That muscle is so sensitive. It may be comparable to using crusty lips, a dry tongue, and sharp fingernails during oral sex.

7. ADDED STIMULATION: Well, let's just stick with the basics. So just continue to rotate #4-#7. Have fun and pay attention to your husbands' reactions.

TIP: I don't know many people who use their teeth while eating ice cream, popsicles, dreamsicles, or ice cream bars. Most teeth are too sensitive. Handle the lollipop as you handle your own sensitive teeth.

8. Now you (and your husband) should be just about ready to burst, meaning your vagina should be moistened. If not, make sure you have some type of lubrication or that wet the lollipop really well. Climb on top of him, in Cowgirl position, and slide down the lollipop. For the best position to make you orgasm or lube more, GRIND - move your body back and forth on him, instead of up and down. You may also be able to position your body to where your clitoris is stimulated by grinding against his pelvic area.

9. Turn around. Now you should be in the Reverse Cowgirl position – straddled on top of your husband, your body should facing his feet, stick your butt out and twerk. You are also able to twerk in the Doggy style position. ADDED STIMULATION: While grinding in reverse cowgirl position, massage his kiwis. "Be his freak!"

10. Remember, this is your husband and GOD gave you two SEX as a wedding gift you are licensed to experiment, experience, enjoy, and "MINISTER" to your husband! **HAVE FUN!**

SOCIAL MEDIA SURVEY

Ladies, what's a #1 need in a relationship?

Top 3 Answers:

1. Communication - Talk to me, Make love to me, Compliment me, Help me with the kids, Hold my hand, spend time with our family, and Show me your love, Stand up for me...

2. Honesty - Tell me the truth! Even if you're wrong, respect me enough to BE HONEST! I have to at least respect your honest.

3. Trust - When I trust you, I feel safe and secure. Be who you say you are, be loyal, Do what you say you're going to do. "Let your yes mean yes, and your no mean no."

Men, what's a #1 need in a relationship?

Top 3 Answers:

1. PEACE – Proverbs 25:24 NLT It's better to live alone in the corner of an attic than with a quarrelsome wife in a lovely home. Let me watch sports without conversation. Give me space when needed, encourage me... NO NAGGING
2. RESPECT – Be my friend, not my mother. Don't try to control me, Notice my efforts
3. LOYALTY - Don't entertain other men.

CHAPTER 21

LINKED IN

As I stated before, the advantage of having a Big Penis is, of course, well-endowed bragging rights and you KNOW that you work with a polish sausage link or kielbasa sausage link. But, you have to be patient and know how to use that big thing to still give MAXIMUM (pun intended) pleasure, along with pleasurable pain. DISADVANTAGE: It's "Too Big." If you have a "too big," or hanging sausage, really big can cause more pain than pleasure; therefore, it can be a turn-off. Nothing is more painful than the feeling of a homemade hysterectomy or inside carpet burn. But, if you know how to use it, work it, with-ya-big-headed self.

Now, those of you who are working with the breakfast sausage links or Li'l Smokies links, **do not feel bad; you are still in the league.** In addition to having to giving multiples (wink), the advantage of working with links is that many women prefer it because it has just enough girth, and many times it will rub the G-spot with each stroke, therefore, causing **MULTIPLE** orgasms. Also, short links, can cause your thrusting to work in your favor because your close contact with the clitoris can cause vaginal AND clitoral orgasms. YES LAWD!!!

Rather it's a link or a sausage you have to be willing to listen to feedback and be open to give the most pleasurable experience as possible. Too big can be painful, too little may not give enough feeling.

Fast or slow does not matter, it's the "motion of the ocean."

MOTION OF THE OCEAN

Rather fast or slow, find the rhythm that her body responds to. There are times you want to make love, and there are times she wants it rough; be in tuned. Find the rhythm for what her body is needing for that moment. Slow Love-making between husband and wife is spiritual, intimate, and sensual. It's an art, a ministry, a moment of oneness. Fast strokes are intense, fun, and even naughty. ;)

What's sad? Women live and die without ever knowing their G-spot. Black men are known for being well-endowed, that's no secret but the experience is everything the older you get. The feeling of having a massage INSIDE the kitten, is amazing. "At a certain age, it's not about huffing, puffing, pain, screaming, scratching and 'Who's ya daddy' anymore. Although that can be fun at times, the beauty is the rhythm, the art..." That type of passion is erotic.

After my first vaginal orgasm experience (close to 40), I began to ask many women about their experiences. Sadly, many woman either hadn't experienced a vaginal orgasm, some weren't sure or had no idea as to what I was talking about; but was curious. We can think a man is good, until we experience better.

Only 10 percent of women easily **climax**. Most women are in the remaining 80-90 percent. I see many women in my practice who feel relief just to know they are "normal" when they have **trouble** climaxing with just vaginal sex but can **climax** with direct clitoral stimulation.

(Holly L. Thacker, 2014).

https://health.clevelandclinic.org/2014/06/help-for-women-who-cant-easily-orgasm/

CHAPTER 22

ART

Okay, there are hundreds of sex positions, so we will just discuss the basics: missionary, doggy-style, spoon, rodeo, and deep stick.

Wives, when you and your husband are in the missionary position, this is your opportunity to enjoy your massage inside out. However, stay engaged and express yourself. Men like to look at you while he makes love to you. Many of them even like to watch their pig go in and out of your warm blanket. So express yourself. In any of these positions, if you normally keep your eyes closed, every now and then, open them and look at him. If you are feeling pleasure, give your Oooh, Mmmh, and Aaahs. Maybe call him a pet name. Tell him how you're feeling (don't go off into no real conversation, keep it sexy.) Use your hands: grab his buttocks, grab the back of his head. When you are making love, make it passionate.

Husbands, don't be selfish. Please don't let her go to bed hot and bothered. Allow her to be pleased before you cum. FOR REAL!!! We all know you will get yours and call it a night but be passionate even if she doesn't orgasm, stay in her head. Tell her how you feel, look into her eyes, hold her hands, and kiss her. GIVE THE MAN MOANS, IT'S A TURN

ON!!! And for the sake of your manhood and your marriage, please don't sound like no tramp!!!!!!!!!

If you are making love to her, keep it passionate.

CHAPTER 23

THE ARTIST

The 80/20 rule of Relationships

Okay, marriage is like music. If you buy an artist's CD, there are some songs that you will like and some that you won't like. When you bought the CD, you bought into the notion that because you like the artist or one song, that you will like all the songs; however, that is not the case. Every song will not be a favorite but most won't throw away the CD for the bad songs. Usually, you fast forward, to you the next song on the CD.

In the beginning, you will not know the words to the artist's songs, just bits and pieces; but, you will **learn** them the more **time** you spend **listening** to it.

There will always be another artist, that has a better voice, that has more moves, or showmanship, but not every artist have the power to move your soul, speak to your spirit, make you cry, or make you want to fall in love. Many times you can tell an artist who sings from experience and one who just have talent. Not all artists are entertainers, but not all fans need entertainment to be entertained; but, these are things you should know **before** you purchase a ticket to their concert.

Know, learn or relearn your artist. This way, you will know their song.

OKAY, LET'S RECAP:

- ✓ MARRIAGE IS NOT HARD, BUT WORK
- ✓ BE SPONTANEOUS
- ✓ ENJOY THE "MAP"
- ✓ EXPERIMENT
- ✓ LAUGH
- ✓ MAKE LOVE
- ✓ HAVE QUICKIES
- ✓ KEEP THE LIGHTS ON
- ✓ HAVE PET NAMES
- ✓ EXPLORE
- ✓ BE CREATIVE
- ✓ TRY SOMETHING NEW
- ✓ ROLE PLAY
- ✓ READ THE SONG OF SOLOMON ;)
- ✓ MAKE NOISES
- ✓ MAKE MEMORIES
- ✓ DATE
- ✓ HAVE A NIGHT CAP
- ✓ BE HIS FREAK
- ✓ BE HER BIG DADDY
- ✓ WOMEN: TAKE IT
- ✓ STEP OUT OF THE BOX
- ✓ LET GO

USE YOUR GOD-GIVEN WEDDING GIFT AND MINISTER TO YOUR SPOUSE BECAUSE GOD SAID,

IT'S GOOD!!!

ENJOY!!!!!!!!!!!!!!!

Looks like there may be a <u>TABOO II!!!!!!!!</u>

TOPICS:

1. The **art** of making Love
2. My medication is causing impotence and my wife doesn't understand.
3. I hated the way I looked after the mastectomy.
4. How we made it, even with family: mama, baby-mama/daddy, step children, and the in-laws.
5. "Being creative." (wink)
6. Recovering from infidelity
7. Recovering from being around at the block
8. Their insecurity vs my insecurity

Also, one thing I can NOT stand is when I ask a couple who's been married for some time, "What's the secret to staying marred __ years?"

Holy Rollers: "GOD," "CHRIST," "Keeping God first."

Then I ask: "Okay, after the cliché, what kept you two together?"

I don't say that to be mean but **THE CHURCH** DIVORCE RATE IS AT 50%. So give me the how to when satan came to the door, when money got funny, when kids cut up, affairs, sickness, disagreements, when the flesh became weak and you thought about throwing in the towel. I mean come on now; the Bible says, "Faith without works is dead." So come on with the real!

In the meantime, Get Ready for New Release...

THE BATTLE is the aftermath of THE DIVORCE.

"Now that the divorce is over, the fighting should die down," the Judge assured. But, was she ever so wrong! The man I loved, and who once loved me, began to treat me with hate: Countless police calls, reports, text messages, etc. A nightmare continued.

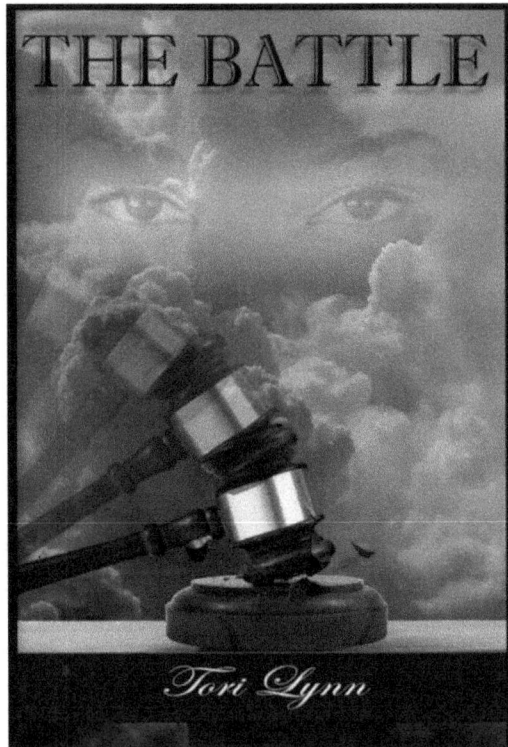

February 22, 2013 – **TORI LYNN**

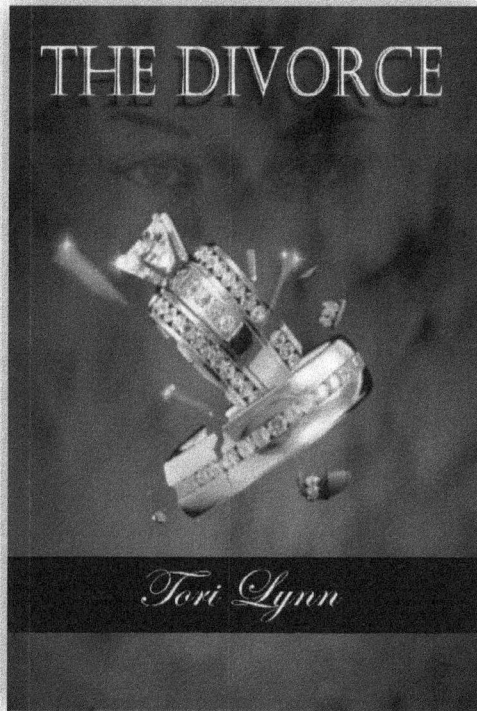

Sex brought them together; Drama tore them apart. Tori speaks about the magical way her and her ex-husband met in church, to the back and forth drama, the family drama, the post-partum depression, and the thoughts of suicide.

Losing everything and facing hardship, trials, and tribulations caused the birthing of her autobiography "The Divorce" as she began to write about her experiences, while empathizing with others' pain. Tori candidly share both the pain and the loss of her faith in family, man, and God. The thought of suicide became an option; but God, who she later realized had never left her. She wants others to know that God has not left them so, *LIVE*!

BIOGRAPHY

Tori Lynn is an author, filmmaker, and inspirational speaker dedicated to speaking to men and women who are facing, going or has gone through a divorce or hardship based on <u>The Divorce</u>. She speaks on how her Faith in God caused her to become successful such as enabling her to buy two homes, drive nice cars and travel while only working three days a week. Tori loved the confidence in being able to buy whatever she desired because of an A+ credit rating. Tori is aware of her highly favored and blessed life.

Tori's best-selling autobiography, "The Divorce" landed her as a guest on Trinity Broadcast Network, countless speaking, radio, and hosting engagements.

She was moved to write "Taboo," because of the rise of divorces, and the disconnect between the church and the world. She was also inspired by Tommy Ford, who captured her vision and their mutual love for marriage & family, while they filmed her short- film, "The Divorce."

Tori obtained a Bachelor of Science in Business Administration in three years, graduating in 2000. While pursuing her degree, she was enrolled full-time in school to be a barber/stylist. She was born and raised in Oklahoma City, Oklahoma and in 2002, Dallas, Texas became her new home where she lived for 17 years. As of 2016 she moved to Atlanta, GA where she resided with her two. Tori became a 2018 New Year's Day Newly Wed.

Tori is also the proud mother of singers, actresses, entrepreneur, and authors Erin Lynn, 9 "Mommy and Daddy are getting a divorce," and Ryan Lynn, 8, "My Feelings Matter."

For speaking engagements contact:

Tori Lynn
214-997-4077
AuthorToriLynn.com
YouAre@TheLynnses.com

www.AuthorToriLynn.com

YouTube.com/AuthorToriLynn

Facebook.com/AuthorToriLynn

ERIN LYNN

MOMMY AND DADDY
ARE GETTING A
DIVORCE

by
Erin Lynn

Erin Lynn is the author of **Mommy and Daddy are getting a Divorce**. This book will give children a voice and/or the ability to relate to another child who's gone through the same experience.

Excerpts: "Mommy Please don't talk about my daddy."

"Daddy, please don't forget about me once you're gone."

RYAN LYNN

Ryan Lynn, is the author of **My Feelings Matter**. Sometimes big people forget that when they are going through a divorce, US CHILDREN ARE TOO and we have feelings. Sometimes we don't know how to express what we are feeling but this book will be our art work of feelings.